How to Learn Mandarin: Tips for Beginners

CHRIS MORGAN

ISBN: 1515270351
ISBN-13: 978-1515270355

CONTENTS

1 INTRODUCTION

<u>Why Mandarin?</u>

Having picked up this book, you have begun a very exciting journey: the journey of learning Mandarin. You could be starting completely from scratch. You may have already managed to learn a little of this beautiful and intriguing language. Either way, in this book I set out lots of hints and tips on both where to start and how to progress your language learning.

There are plenty of good reasons to learn Mandarin. Perhaps you are interested in the culture, the art, the calligraphy, the music, the history, or the politics of China. Perhaps you come into contact with Mandarin speakers in a social or business context. Perhaps you are simply interested in learning the language that has more native speakers than any other language on our planet. Perhaps you just need a new hobby!

As the Chinese proverb says, *"To learn a language*

is to have one more window from which to look at the world." Or, in Chinese:

学一门语言，就是多一个观察世界的窗户

I am sure that at some point in the future this phrase will easily trip off your tongue! By the end of this book, you will already know two of these characters.

Why is Mandarin different?

When you first start, Mandarin can look like a rather bewildering language. In particular, there are two main areas of difficulty for beginners:

(i) Tones

Mandarin is a "tonal" language. The way that you raise or lower your voice as you speak changes the meaning of what you say.

For example, "ma" said in a high and level tone means "mother". But use a lower, falling and rising tone and it means horse. This could lead to a tricky situation if meeting Mandarin speaking in-laws for the first time!

After you have had a bit of practice listening to some Mandarin phrases, you will be surprised at how soon you start to recognise the tones. I will explain tones more in chapter 5.

(ii) Characters

Chinese characters at first approach for me were

intriguing and challenging in equal amounts. Add to that the fact that they can be written vertically or horizontally and it can feel like you have bitten off more than you can chew. But, don't panic. As you find out more about how the characters are formed, they become surprisingly easy to learn. For example:

This looks like somebody standing with their legs apart – and in fact it means "man" or "person". There you go, you can now read one Chinese character already! You will learn how to get started with characters in chapter 6.

As with learning any language, there are difficult aspects and there are easier aspects. You should certainly not be put off by thinking that Mandarin is "too difficult".

Where to start?

I have been learning Mandarin for a few years now. For me, the big attraction was how different it was to the European languages I have learnt before. It seemed like a challenge. I am also a bit of a technology fan, so it seemed like a good opportunity to try out some of the great new websites and apps for language learners.

There is no 'one size fits all' approach to learning a language. What works for one person could be a waste of time for another. I do not promise that by the end of reading this book you will be fluent in Mandarin. But I will pass on some really useful hints, tips and techniques that have helped me to get to grips with the basics, including:

- how to come up with an achievable language learning strategy;

- how to find an evening class, private tutor, or language exchange partner (and how to get the most out of them); and

- how to find and use the best language learning materials (including books, CDs, traditional courses, websites, apps and YouTube channels).

This book will also give you an introduction to:

- the sounds of the Mandarin language;

- written Chinese characters; and

- how to learn Mandarin vocabulary and grammar.

I have also included a glossary at the back, which sets out some of the key words used in this book.

You will be surprised at how much progress you can make in a short space of time, even if you do not have hours each day to devote to language learning. Little and often is surprisingly effective.

How to use this book

Use this book like a personal trainer. Read a chapter, try something out, and then pick up the book again. That way you will keep your learning fresh. To get you going, at the end of each chapter I have included some "what next?" tasks for you to try. The important thing is that you try out the many resources and materials available to see what works for you.

By the time you get to the end of this book, aim to:

1. have established a regular routine for learning Mandarin, using a variety of interesting resources and materials;

2. be able to write some common characters (I will show you that this is not as difficult as you might think);

3. be able to construct some basic sentences (I will provide you with plenty of examples of resources you can use to learn some of these); and

4. have had a basic conversation with a native Mandarin speaker (I will give you some tips on how to find one).

By the time you reach the end of this book, you will have plenty of ideas about how to progress your learning of Mandarin. Above all, I hope you have as much fun learning Mandarin as I have.

Good luck!

2 YOUR LANGUAGE LEARNING STRATEGY

When you decide to learn a new language, it is important to consider three things at the outset: setting a goal; getting a routine; and choosing the right learning materials. I will cover the last of these in the next chapter. Together, these three things will provide a framework for your language-learning activities and will ensure that you stay on track.

Setting a goal

First, consider why you would like to learn Mandarin. Perhaps you would like to be able to read a menu at your local Chinese restaurant, 'get by' as a tourist on holiday, or be able to use Mandarin in a business context. Thinking about why you are learning Mandarin will help you work out what to focus on.

If your goal is to be able to read a menu in Chinese, focus on learning how to read the written characters and learning food related vocabulary.

If your goal is to be able to use the language on holiday, make sure you get some speaking and listening practice and that you also learn words and phrases relating to directions, money, visiting attractions, and staying in a hotel.

If your goal is to be able to use the language for business, focus to begin with on how to start and end a 'polite' conversation (including greetings and forms of addressing somebody you do not know) and on key industry-related vocabulary.

If you have several goals, take one at a time – don't worry about starting with the easiest first. If you can see common vocabulary or skill areas to target, you might want to prioritise those first.

You should choose a target that is specific and achievable. For example, if you are travelling to China, set yourself two weeks to learn to pronounce five different attractions or public buildings and to recognise their written characters.

Once you have achieved your first target, go back to your overall goal and focus on the next thing you need to learn to achieve it.

Make sure that your goal is realistic and that you do not try to do too much in too short a period of time. If you expect to be able to read a Chinese newspaper, or discuss the finer points of Chinese philosophy, in two weeks' time, you are going to be disappointed.

In three or six months, however, you could aim to have a basic understanding of greetings, know how to talk about yourself and your family, count to 100 (there is a pattern that is easy to learn!), and be familiar with basic vocabulary relating to a few particular topics. If you can stick to your small targets towards this bigger goal, you can be rightly proud of yourself!

<u>Getting a routine</u>

Having thought about your goal for learning Mandarin, the next step is to establish a routine that will make sure you are regularly learning and practising the language. Think about what resources you will use (see chapter 4 for inspiration) and how to fit in your learning with your lifestyle.

Over the years, I have found that finding an evening class or private tutor to go to on a weekly or fortnightly basis has given me an anchor for my language-learning routine. I always knew that I needed to prepare for the lesson to get the most out of it and this gave me a regularly occurring deadline to work towards. I could then fit my learning in the gaps in my timetable, using the most suitable resources possible.

For example, if I had some free time in an evening, I would practice using books – but if I was squeezing in a short session of learning on my commute I would use an app on the bus or a CD in the car. To be sociable at lunchtime, I would meet up with a language exchange partner.

I will go into more detail on how you can get stuck into all of these fun language-learning activities in the coming chapters.

What next?

1. Write down your goal for learning Mandarin.

2. Come up with one specific and achievable target to achieve within two weeks.

3. Start to think creatively about how you can fit language-learning into your weekly schedule. Do you commute to work? Do you have spare time at lunchtime or on particular evenings? Remember, being able to study a little and often is the key!

3 CLASSES, PRIVATE TUTORS AND EXCHANGE PARTNERS

It is very important to be guided in your learning by someone experienced in the language. You will have someone to practise with, to correct your mistakes, to encourage you and to answer your questions.

<u>Evening classes</u>

I began learning Mandarin in an evening class, which had its good and bad points.

Positives: an evening class provides a regular structure to your learning – and having paid for a class, you feel motivated to turn up and make the most of it. It is also nice to have contact with some fellow language learners. Courses are often 8 to 10 weeks long and follow school terms.

Negatives: classes can be rather inflexible to individual learners' goals, preferred style of learning and speed. One person may have learnt some Mandarin before and be familiar with how to speak the language. One person may be quite artistic and have tried their hand at Chinese calligraphy. One person may have already learnt five languages and be able to pick things up very quickly. One person may be new to language learning and need to take things more slowly.

You might find an evening class a good opportunity to try new things, or you might find it distracting. If you do choose to try one, a lot will come down to the skill of the teacher in bringing the class together and providing interesting and clear exercises and explanations of materials.

The teacher of the evening class I attended was very passionate about Chinese culture, which made her lessons very engaging. However, I sometimes felt that we jumped around resources and subjects, making the lessons sometimes rather confusing.

To find an evening class taking place near you, contact a school or college close to where you live, or pop into your local library (where courses are often advertised on notice boards). Sometimes local councils will also be able to point you in the right direction.

Attending an evening class is definitely worth a try, but do not be disheartened if it turns out not to be a learning environment for you.

Private tutors

Alternatively, or in addition to an evening class (if

you are particularly keen), I would thoroughly recommend finding a local private tutor. There is nothing like face-to-face lessons once a week, or once a fortnight, to really improve your familiarity with a language and your ability to speak it. This way you can really focus on things you find difficult, or things you would particularly like to learn. Having one-to-one attention from a native speaker is also by far the best way to work on your pronunciation and spoken language.

I have had two different private tutors, both were very good. The first was a young mother on maternity leave and the second was a university student. Both provided invaluable native speaker input into my Mandarin learning. Both were also very interesting people to speak with more generally about China and Chinese culture.

I found my tutors on www.uktutors.com, but you can also try searching for a tutor on your local version of the "Gumtree" website (if you are in the UK) or by conducting an internet search for "Mandarin tutor in X" - there will doubtless be various options to consider.

Alternatively, you could find a language tutor prepared to give lessons over Skype, for instance via the website:

www.italki.com

Many language learners swear by this website, where you should have no problem finding a native speaker willing to teach you at a reasonable rate.

Conversation exchange partners

You can also use www.italki.com to find a conversation exchange partner, if you wish – i.e. you speak with them partly in English and partly in Mandarin.

It is certainly worth finding a native speaker to practice with, and if you can do this for free (in exchange for giving somebody a bit of English language assistance) then so much the better.

I have tried various conversation exchanges, with varying success. The following website is also a good place to find language exchange partners:

www.conversationexchange.com

Preparing for your sessions

To get the most out of a language exchange, it is best to ensure that you try to have structured conversations or structured reading practice. I would recommend taking along your textbook, a reading book, or some other written material that you can discuss and use to practice speaking. I know from personal experience that there is nothing worse than staring blankly into a cup of coffee, having exhausted all of the words and phrases that you can think of on the spur of the moment!

If you do opt for a 'taught' method of learning Mandarin, this does not mean that you can sit back and let someone else take charge! It is important to get into a regular routine of preparation and learning to fully benefit. It is better to do a little often rather than trying to cram a week's work into the 30 minutes before your next lesson! You will be very surprised how much progress you make if you can set aside just 15 minutes per day to practice exercises, learn some vocab, or read some relevant materials.

What next?

1. Use the internet to locate nearby evening classes.

2. Register on the "Conversation Exchange" website (www.conversationexchange.com) and on Italki (www.italki.com) and browse these sites for options for language exchange partners – whether based locally to you or via Skype.

3. If all else fails, see whether there is a Mandarin speaker in your local community who might be able to help you!

4 CHOOSING THE RIGHT LEARNING MATERIALS

If you choose to attend an evening class, or use a private tutor, it is likely that your tutor will suggest a textbook for you to purchase. Of course, even if they do, there is nothing stopping you from purchasing other books to use as well – I am somebody who likes to have a variety of books to dip into, and you may also like this approach too.

As a first step, it is always worth checking out what resources your local library has to offer. This might include audio CDs (or even cassettes, if you can locate a cassette player!) as well as books. It is a good way to "try before you buy". Your local library is also likely to be able to source books (at little or no cost to you) from elsewhere in your area – so if they don't seem to have any Mandarin related materials, do make sure you ask at the information desk.

Other than this, it is surprising what unusual gems

you might find in your local charity stores. I managed to pick up a set of "Winnie the Pooh" books written in traditional Chinese characters! Of course, bookshops are also great places to browse for inspiration.

I will now talk you through some of the books I have found most useful.

Mandarin language textbooks

I attended a couple of classes where the tutor recommended "*Easy Peasy Chinese: Mandarin Chinese for Beginners*" by Elinor Greenwood (published by DK). This comes with a CD and has very clear explanations and text. It is aimed at children, but if that doesn't bother you then it is actually quite a useful and informative book. It is certainly a good place to start for complete beginners.

More recently, I have been working through "*Teach Yourself Beginner's Mandarin Chinese*" by Elizabeth Scurfield and Lianyi Song (published by Teach Yourself). This is a 'classic' style book to learn Mandarin and it is useful and thorough, but a few words of warning:

> (a) it uses only "Pinyin", i.e. Mandarin written in the Western (Latin) alphabet rather than in Chinese characters (I'll explain more about this in chapter 5), so I would only recommend using this book if you have a very patient tutor, as I have been lucky enough to have, who is willing to teach you all the Chinese characters as you go along;

and

(b) it is a challenging book for a complete beginner; however, I would certainly recommend the book and I do feel that it is worth the effort in order to get a really thorough grounding in the basics and to take you through towards an intermediate level and beyond.

As well as using a formal textbooks, I would recommend you look at some of the other materials available that focus on particular areas of study.

Books about writing Chinese characters

- "*Chineasy: The New Way to Read Chinese*" by ShaoLan. This is an imaginative and great-looking book that aims to make learning Chinese characters easy via a "new visual method" created by the author. It teaches you to recognise the shapes of characters by presenting them with cartoon drawings around them to help you remember the meaning. It also provides information on how groups of similar characters are related.

- "*Fun with Chinese Characters*" published by Marshall Cavendish. There are three volumes in this series and it is possible to buy them as a set. The books are really good. They aim to "demystify" Chinese characters and they do just that, showing how the characters evolved from ancient picture-based representations. Also included is a stroke-by-stroke guide on how to write the characters, along with entertaining cartoons that make the characters memorable. In addition, the first volume begins with some interesting historical background.

- "*Learn to Write Chinese Characters*" by Johan Björkstén. This is published by Yale University Press, so it is fairly academic – however, it is perfectly accessible and it contains very interesting historical background to Chinese characters and different forms of Chinese calligraphy. The section that I found most useful was a guide to around thirty of the most common "radicals" (an important part of Chinese characters which I will explain more in chapter 6) and some examples of characters that use them. You will gain a lot of knowledge by reading through this book and writing out the characters used in the examples.

- "*Read and Write Chinese Script*" published by Teach Yourself. In the Teach Yourself series, this book focusses solely on reading and writing Chinese characters. It contains information about the origins of the characters, how the characters are formed, how to write the characters (by explaining the basic strokes to use). It moves on to teach you about the characters commonly used in everyday situations, from place signs to menus, tickets and newspaper weather forecasts.

Phrasebooks and audio materials

- "*Mandarin Chinese Phrase Book & CD*" published by Berlitz. This is a handy little book that lists phrases and vocabulary around key topics, from "travel survival" to "food and drink", "people", "leisure time", "special requirements" and "emergency". The CD will help you with pronunciation. The book is aimed at those travelling to China for business or pleasure, but it is a useful reference book for anybody learning Mandarin.

- "*Rapid Mandarin Chinese, Volume 1*" (Earworms: Musical Brain Trainer). This is a spoken audio CD, with words and phrases spoken over gentle music, which is relaxing and effective in equal measure! It is surprising how memorable words spoken in Mandarin become when there is music in the background. This is a great CD to listen to on the bus or in the car.

Books about Chinese culture

- "*Chinese Language and Culture: Your essential guide to Mandarin and life in modern China*" published by Collins. This is an interesting book if you are interested not just in the Chinese language itself but also subjects such as etiquette, Chinese names, festivals, food, philosophy, and artistic traditions.

Dictionaries

I have a copy of the Collins Pocket Oxford English-Chinese / Chinese-English dictionary, which is comprehensive and clearly laid-out. However, as a beginner it can be difficult to use a 'normal' dictionary to look up a Chinese character.

To get around this issue, I would very strongly recommend that you download the "Pleco" dictionary app, which at the time of writing is available for free in both the Android and iPhone app stores. This app has a very clever feature that enables you to look up characters by simply drawing them on the screen, which very useful for the beginner wanting to practice writing characters!

More of this later – in chapter 7 I will come to apps, websites, and e-books that you can use to enhance your study of Mandarin.

<u>What next?</u>

1. Visit your local library and search the catalogue for "Mandarin" and "China". Try to find one book about the Mandarin language, one book about China, and one book written in Chinese for you to use to simply look at the characters.

2. Pick a book from the list above to try. Order it into your local library, or browse in a local bookshop, if you would like to 'try before you buy'.

5 INTRODUCTION TO THE MANDARIN LANGUAGE: PINYIN AND TONES

There are nearly a billion people who speak Mandarin across much of northern and south-western China. It is the sole official national language in China and Taiwan and one of four official languages in Singapore. Mandarin is also one of the most frequently used dialects of Chinese spoken by Chinese communities living abroad and is one of the six official languages of the United Nations.

For English speakers wanting to learn Mandarin, there are two new concepts to understand at the start, before learning anything else: "Pinyin" and the "tones". I will now explain each of these in turn.

<u>Pinyin</u>

"Pinyin" is a system of writing down Mandarin using

our Western (Latin) alphabet, showing how the words are actually spoken. If you find Chinese characters unfamiliar or tricky, it is a much easier way of reading Chinese.

For example, the character for "I" is quite complicated:

In Pinyin, this is written, "wǒ", which is how it sounds. (The accent over the "o" indicates the tone; I will explain this in the next section of this chapter.)

Although Chinese newspapers and books are written using characters, Pinyin is a useful place to start for the beginner. Pinyin is not just used by foreigners to learn Mandarin, but it is also used to teach schoolchildren in mainland China. It is important to learn to read Pinyin, as it provides a way of reading and writing Mandarin without having to use Chinese characters and is a good "introduction" to the language.

Many sounds in Pinyin are the same as in English so, for example, "ma" is pronounced exactly as you would expect.

The following consonants, however, are not pronounced the same as in English:
j, q, x, z, c, s, zh, ch, sh, and r

It is difficult to explain in writing how these sounds

should be pronounced. Some books try to do this with diagrams of the mouth and throat, but it is probably much easier if you hear a native speaker saying them – either a teacher or tutor, or on a CD that accompanies your textbook. If you search for "Chinese Pinyin" on YouTube, you will also be able to find some handy video demonstrations. If you are having private lessons, or a language exchange, make sure that your tutor or exchange partner takes the time to teach you Pinyin so that you become comfortable with the sounds of Mandarin.

As you become familiar with Pinyin, make sure that you also start to learn the corresponding Chinese characters as well. Beware of books that only use Pinyin, unless you have a teacher able to teach you the characters for the words used. Think of Pinyin as being a way into the "spoken" Mandarin language; if you wish to progress to intermediate level and beyond, you will need to start learning how Chinese characters are written (and I will come onto this in more detail in the next chapter).

Tones

Mandarin is a "tonal" language. This means that the pitch of your voice (high or low), and whether your voices rises or falls as you are saying something, can change the meaning of what you are saying. This means that you need to make sure that you learn tones as you learn words, right from the start. It will be much harder to have to go back and learn them later on if you neglect to do this!

There are four different "tones" in Mandarin. By way

of example, here is how they are written with the word "ma":

- First tone: mā (also can be written "ma1") – a high, continuous tone (meaning of mā = mother)

- Second tone: má (or "ma2") – a rising tone (meaning of má = hemp)

- Third tone: mǎ (or "ma3") – a falling and then rising tone (meaning of mǎ = horse)

- Fourth tone: mà (or "ma4") – an abruptly falling tone (meaning of mà = scold)

You can see from the above the wide range of meanings that a word can have, depending upon how you pronounce it! So, it is worth taking the time to really get familiar with the tones. The accents used over the vowels to show which tone to use look like the shape of the sound you need to make. This will help you to remember how to pronounce a word.

There is also what is called a "neutral" tone, a tone that is said gently and without a particular pitch:

- Neutral tone: ma (or "ma5") – an 'unpitched' tone (meaning of ma = when used at the end of a sentence, indicates a question)

"Hold on," I hear you say, "I thought you said there were four tones in Mandarin!" Yes, you are absolutely right. The "neutral tone" is not thought of as being like the other four, which all involve using pitch or change in pitch in your voice (so that it almost sounds like you are singing). The "neutral tone" is said fleetingly, as if (as an English speaker) you are just saying it normally and without any "singing" quality to your voice.

I have tried to briefly describe how the tones sound above, but you need to hear how they sound: search YouTube for "Mandarin tones" to find a demonstration and then re-read the above section of this chapter again for explanation. Have a go at copying them. I have found that when you are walking to work is an excellent time to practice speaking the tones, if you don't mind startling the odd passer-by!

Do not panic if you do not feel that you can pronounce the tones properly at first, or even after months of learning. It is a skill that takes time to develop and in the meantime you should not let it put you off trying to speak Mandarin. More times than not, a native speaker will understand what you are trying to say even if you do not use the correct tones.

What next?

1. **Pinyin**: Visit the BBC "Real Chinese" website and work through a few of the different sections, which have audio examples to give you a feel for the sounds of the Mandarin language whilst teaching you some basic words and phrases, such as greetings, and how they are written in Pinyin:

2. **Tones**: Search YouTube for "Chinese Crosstalk" – a form of comedy usually involving two people, based very heavily on the use of language for comic effect. Clearly as a beginner, you will not be able to understand what is being said (so try to find videos with English subtitles if you wish to do so!), but just use the videos to enable you to listen to the "sound-world" of the Mandarin language. Because language is so important to this form of comedy (which usually involves lots of puns), the tones of the words are often strongly emphasised by the speakers – meaning that it is good material to listen to in order to become familiar with the tones of Mandarin.

6 INTRODUCTION TO CHINESE CHARACTERS

Do you remember the character you learnt in the introduction to this book:

This looks like somebody standing with their legs apart and means "man" or "person".

I will now teach you a second character. What might a person with their arms outstretched mean?

This character means "big".

You can now read two characters! I bet you will be surprised that it is not nearly so difficult to learn Chinese characters as you might have thought.

Here are three more characters for you to have a look at:

Yes, you've guessed it: these are the characters for the numbers "one", "two", and "three". Nice and easy!

Now that we are on a roll, let's look at three slightly more complicated characters. These seem overwhelming at first, but can you spot a common element in each of these three characters? Hint: it's on the left hand side of each one:

Can you see that there is a squashed up and slightly rotated version of the "man/person" character we learnt earlier? This shows that each of these three characters has something to do with a person.

The characters mean "you", "you" (the polite form), and "he" respectively. The use of the squashed up "man/person" character in each of them is known as the "**radical**", a specific "building block" that each character has that often indicates the meaning of the character.

Being able to recognise the radical used in a character will not only often give you a hint as to the character's meaning but it will also enable you to look up the character in a traditional Chinese dictionary, which tend to list characters by radical and number of strokes. For instance, to look up the "you" character, you would firstly have to know that it contains the "man" radical and secondly that it contains five other strokes. You would look up this combination in the index to a dictionary and it would tell you what page to look on to find the meaning of the character.

As a beginner, don't worry too much about this – but it is always worth knowing what is in store for you as your Mandarin learning progresses!

Now that you have seen eight characters, you are hopefully beginning to get a feel for the fact that, despite looking very complicated, there are patterns in Chinese characters. Spotting these will help you to remember the characters more easily.

Things start getting even more interesting when you learn that the characters for "woman" and "child", when combined together into one character, mean "good".

Woman:

女

Child:

子

Good:

好

When you squint at them, the character for woman almost looks like a woman curtseying and the character for child almost looks like a stick baby – and the fact that these combine to mean "good" paints a nice image that means that the character for "good" is easy to remember.

Let's look at two characters whose meaning does not jump out at you at first glance:

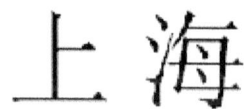

But look again at the characters. The first character has a small horizontal line above a larger horizontal line. It means "upon".

The second character has three "drops" on its left-hand side (the bottom one looks a bit smeared), which indicate that it is something to do with water. This is the water "radical", to use the technical term I mentioned above. In fact, this character means "sea".

Taken together, the characters literally mean "upon sea" and in Mandarin they are pronounced Shàng-hǎi. In other words, these characters are referring to "Shanghai", the largest city in the world by population and a major port in the Yangtze River Delta in East China.

There are other strategies that you can use to learn characters. For example, take the character:

This arguably looks like the letter "B" over the letter "E", with an extra squiggle. It means the verb "to be".

Now take the character:

This arguably looks like the letter "E" with a squiggle over two letter "G"s, one of which is the wrong way around. It means "egg".

I hope you have the idea that there are rules, patterns and logical explanations lying behind the make-up of characters that can help you to recognise them. You are well on the way to being able to read a good number of Chinese characters already!

In this book, I have been teaching you characters in their "simplified" form. This is the form of characters used in mainland China and in Singapore, promoted by the Chinese government since the 1950s and 1960s in order to improve literacy. In Hong Kong and Taiwan, "traditional" characters are still used. These are more complex than simplified characters, so the simplified characters are certainly the best place to start for any foreigner learning Chinese.

What next?

1. Visit "Learn Chinese Online" - www.learnchineseez.com, click on "Simplified Characters", and you will be taken to an interactive list of 4000

characters listed in order of frequency of use. Click on one you like the look of – and the website will show you how to write it, what it means, and some sample uses. Don't just look at your screen while you are doing this – grab a pen and piece of paper and have a go at writing the character! Going forward, aim to learn perhaps five characters a week, one per weekday, using the weekend to revise and practice what you have learned during the week. You will be surprised at how quickly you start to pick them up.

2.   Find an article online about the difference between "simplified" and "traditional" characters. This will give you interesting insight not only into the way in which the Chinese language is written down, but also into some interesting political and historical issues relating to it.

7 LEARNING VOCABULARY

In order to become familiar with any foreign language you need to learn vocabulary. This sentence is likely to send shudders down the spines of all who remember secondary school language lessons where teachers would present lists of vocab that would have to be memorized for a test - and then probably forgotten as soon as the test was over!

However, learning vocab does not have to be difficult or painful. Believe it or not, it can actually be quite enjoyable. In this chapter I will show you how.

<u>1. Use an appropriate list of vocabulary</u>

To keep your vocabulary learning well-structured try to learn a word a day, using a list of vocabulary based on the goal you have set for your language learning. There is no point learning vocabulary for the sake of it as you are unlikely to remember it.

Pick vocabulary lists that relate to your interests and you will be surprised at how easily the new words stick in your mind.

2. Use music

If words are sung (particularly to a catchy tune!) then they are much more memorable than if you just read them. A very good way to start to become familiar with Mandarin words and phrases is to find and listen to pop songs sung in Mandarin on YouTube with English subtitles.

To get you going, try searching YouTube for "*Pengyou by Zhou HuaJian with lyrics*". You will find a song that uses fairly basic language and a video displaying the lyrics in Chinese characters, Pinyin, and English. There are lots of other such videos on YouTube. Make sure you make the most of this free resource!

3. Use Twitter

There are quite a few accounts on Twitter that it is worth following, to get a "word of the day" or a link to an interesting blog or article, that will help you with your Mandarin learning activities. If you do not have a Twitter account, you can just use the links below to see the accounts online rather than via a Twitter app.

Here are some useful accounts that I would suggest you take a look at:

@learnchinesehl - www.twitter.com/learnchinesehl

@fluentchinese - www.twitter.com/fluentchinese

@allaboutchinese - www.twitter.com/allaboutchinese

@FluentUChinese - www.twitter.com/FluentUChinese

@ChineseGrammar- www.twitter.com/ChineseGrammar

@fluent_mandarin - www.twitter.com/fluent_mandarin

@hanyudotco - www.twitter.com/hanyudotco

@MandarinHQ - www.twitter.com/MandarinHQ

4. Use written materials

As a beginner, reading written materials in Chinese will clearly be a challenge. However, have a look at the Chinese version of the BBC news website:

www.bbc.com/zhongwen/simp

You can take a guess at what the articles are about thanks to the pictures and you can use an online translation service (such as Google Translate) to translate and read the text. Using "authentic" rather than artificial materials can make what you learn more memorable.

Comic books or children's books with pictures are also good to get vocabulary practice. I would advise you to have a browse of the "foreign literature" section when you are next in your local bookshop or library. Don't feel you need to be able to understand everything (or anything!) – as a beginner, it is just a good idea to look at the written language and you will be surprised at how quickly you start to recognise an increasing number of characters.

5. Use e-books

I have enjoyed reading the *"Big Cat and Little Dog: Beginning to Read Mandarin Chinese"* series on my Kindle. Have a look at these if you enjoy simple picture books as they are a very good way of getting some reading practice. These short e-books cost less than £2 each.

6. Use apps

There are an increasing number of smartphone apps designed for language learners, many of which assist with learning vocabulary.

The "Pleco" dictionary app can also be used to create lists of vocabulary and flashcards.

There is also a very useful (and free of charge) app called "Memrise", which you can also access online at:

www.memrise.com

This app and website enable you to learn sets of vocabulary in a foreign language (not just Mandarin) by creating flashcards and then testing you on them. It is based on the idea of "spaced repetition", i.e. when you learn a new word you will need to then see it quite often, but as it becomes part of your longer-term memory you will not need to be reminded of its meaning so often.

Both "Pleco" and "Memrise" are excellent learning

tools. Have a go with these and browse through the appstore for your phone and search for Mandarin-related apps. More are appearing all the time, so there are plenty of options and you can pick something that matches the way in which you prefer to learn.

7. Use satellite or cable TV

When flicking through obscure channels on Sky TV, I discovered channel 785, PCNE Chinese, which broadcasts in Mandarin – often with subtitles, although in Chinese characters only! Even if you know no Mandarin, you will probably be surprised at how much TV you can understand. Many TV shows are in similar formats and it is possible to get the gist of what is being said from facial expressions and hand gestures. If nothing else, listening to Mandarin TV will mean that you become familiar with how the language sounds. The importance of this should not be underestimated.

8. Make your own vocab lists

It is quite easy to find vocabulary lists on the internet, usually organised by subject matter. For example, if you are particularly keen on food and drink and you would like to be able to decode the menu in a Chinese restaurant, search for "Mandarin food and drink vocabulary" and I am sure you will easily be able to find a list of words that you can then write on flashcards and learn over a period of time.

To make flashcards, use roughly business card size pieces of card and write a Chinese character on one side and the English and Pinyin on the reverse. Test yourself at random rather than in sequence, perhaps on five to ten cards per day. Any you do not know, write out ten times by hand on a blank piece of paper. You can buy blank flashcards at most stationary shops. I found a useful set of blank flashcards, connected with a metal ring (so particularly useful for having in your pocket and looking at on a train or bus), at a local Wilkinsons store.

You can use a dictionary or dictionary app, such as "Pleco", and compile your own list of vocabulary in relation to a particular subject of interest. Of course, at this stage, it is more about teaching yourself to recognise characters rather than be able to write them out by memory.

I made a list of vocabulary in relation to technology and to show you how I began, here is the initial list of words I put together:

电脑

= **diànnǎo** (literally "*electric brain*") – computer

= **bǐjìběn diànnǎo** (literally "*notebook electric*

brain") – laptop

平板电脑

= **píngbǎn diànnǎo** (literally "*flat electric brain*") – tablet computer

电子书

= **diànzishū** (literally "electric thing book") – e-book

电子阅读器

= **diànzǐ yuèdúqì** (literally "**electric thing reading device**") – e-reader

网页

= **wǎngyè** (literally "*net page*") – website

数码

= **shùmǎ** (literally "*number code*") – digital

Crucial to remembering the characters and how these words are made up is including a "literal" translation of each word in your list – and this is also actually very interesting as you can see, in the case of the technology related words above, how the Mandarin language has developed to cope with new things and concepts. There is often a clear logic to how words are formed. What is a computer, after all, if not an electric brain!

What next?

1. If you don't mind looking at materials aimed at children (which are usually more fun than those aimed at adults), have a look at the BBC Schools, Mandarin Vocabulary website:

www.bbc.co.uk/schools/primarylanguages/mandarin

2. Sign up (for free) and have a play with the "Memrise" smartphone app or website:

www.memrise.com

3. Download and play with "Pleco". Try looking up the character for person that we learnt

earlier:

To write the character, you write the sweep down to the left first, then the sweep down to the right.

4. Search the internet for "*Mandarin vocabulary lists*" and focus on something that matches a personal interest of yours, whether animals, politics, or food and drink. Try looking at some of the characters and try to write them out.

8 LEARNING GRAMMAR

Despite Mandarin being seen as a "difficult" language for English speakers to master, the good news is that the grammar is not actually very difficult at all.

For instance, verbs ("doing words") do not change depending on who or how many people are doing an action, or when the action was carried out. In other words, when you have learned how to say "I go", you can then use exactly the same word to say "you go", "they went", "we will go", and so on. In each case, in Mandarin the word "qù" would be used for each of these variants of "go".

There are no genders in Mandarin. You may remember learning languages in school and having the headache of having to learn whether a noun takes "le" or "la" in French, "el" or "la" in Spanish, "il" or "la" in Italian, or "der", "die" or "das" in German. So at least from that point of view, Mandarin is an easy language to learn!

Often, single-character words are used in Mandarin for a particular grammatical effect. For example, to show that an action has been completed, you simply say "le" after the verb. So, using the word "go" we learnt above, if you see or hear "qù le" in a sentence, it indicates that the "going" has finished (i.e. "gone").

To indicate that you will do something in the future, you just say "yào" before the verb. Accordingly, "yào qù" can be translated as "will go".

To get a feel for how words such as these, and others, are used in the Mandarin language, the "Chinese Grammar Wiki" website referenced below is excellent and well worth dipping into.

Rather than thinking of grammar as being an endless list of boring rules, think of it as being the patterns used to arrange the words in a language. Just as with learning vocabulary, it is difficult if not impossible to learn grammar out of context.

Natural learning

Use the same techniques to learn grammar as you have learnt to memorise words –try to learn short phrases, seeing how the words fit together.

For example, if you are listening to a song on YouTube with subtitles, once you have become familiar with the words used, try to remember they order they come in. Ask yourself where time-related words (e.g. "now", "yesterday", "next year") tend to fall in a sentence. Where does the verb, the "doing word", appear? What changes if something took place in the past? What about if an action takes place in the future? After listening to and thinking about a few songs in this way, you will quickly start to see patterns emerging.

This is after all how children learn grammar, i.e. not by robotically learning rules. If you listen to a catchy song that means you remember the words for "I", "love", and "you", and you also remember the order these come in, then without knowing it you have learnt to connect a subject, a verb and an object. By listening to other songs and looking at other materials, over time you will gain a feel for how to change the words around, or incorporate other words, so as to be able to say things such as "I love the sun", "you love to travel", and so on. In other words, you are learning the grammar of the language 'organically' and naturally.

Using formal learning resources

As you are working through whichever textbook you have chosen to learn Mandarin, try to think about the way in which phrases and sentences are fitted together. The easiest way to "learn" grammar is often to just get a feel for how words are used with one another, rather than worrying too much about the theoretical rules – at least to begin with.

There is a very useful website, "Chinese Grammar Wiki" (link provided in "What next?" section below), which breaks down Chinese grammar into bite-size chunks and then arranges these by level of difficulty. I would definitely suggest you take at this website, which is an excellent free resource to learn about Chinese grammar in an accessible way.

If you are somebody who likes to read about the formal rules of grammar when learning a new language, then good for you; as I said earlier, there is no 'one size fits all' approach and the important thing is to learn in a way that is interesting and enjoyable for you personally. If you do enjoy detailed and technical explanations of grammar, then "Modern Mandarin Chinese Grammar: A Practical Guide" published by Routledge is highly regarded and probably the only reference text on Chinese grammar that you will ever need.

What next?

1. Visit "Chinese Grammar Wiki" and have a browse:

http://resources.allsetlearning.com/chinese/grammar

2. Visit the YouTube "MVS Mandarin" channel, which has an ever increasing number of excellent, short videos explaining all the key points of Mandarin grammar:

www.youtube.com/user/MandarinIsAwesome

9 ONWARDS AND UPWARDS!

You are now well on the way to learning Mandarin. You have established your goal, set a routine, and decided what materials to use. You have a feel for the basics of the Mandarin language and how Chinese characters are written. Most importantly, you have plenty of materials and ideas to get you going and to put into practice, to keep your language-learning journey structured and interesting.

<u>What next?</u>

1. For further inspiration, take a look at the videos on the "Learn Chinese Now" and "New York Chinese Language Centre" YouTube channels:

   www.youtube.com/user/learnchinesenow

   www.youtube.com/user/NYChineseLearning

2. Go forth and learn Mandarin:

祝你好運

= *zhù nǐ háoyùn* – I wish you good luck!

(If you recognised the characters for "you" and "good" in the above phrase, then you are already doing brilliantly. If not, don't worry; just make sure you keep dipping into the earlier chapters to refresh your memory!)

I hope you have a lot of fun on your exciting journey of learning Mandarin!

10 GLOSSARY

Character: a 'unit' of written Chinese. *Traditional characters* (used in Hong Kong and Taiwan) are more complex than *simplified characters* (used in mainland China and Singapore). Words are usually one, two or three characters long. A character does not correspond with a "letter" of the Western (Latin) alphabet.

(See chapter 6 for more information on characters.)

Pinyin: an official method of writing down Mandarin in the Western (Latin) alphabet. It captures the sounds of spoken Mandarin, though not always with letters that correspond exactly to how letters are pronounced in English.

(See chapter 5 for more information on Pinyin.)

Radical: a "building block" or part of each Chinese character, which often gives a hint as to the meaning of the character.

(See chapter 6 for more information on radicals.)

Tone: the pitch, or change in pitch, used to speak a syllable in Mandarin. There are four distinct tones: 1. high and continuous; 2. rising; 3. falling and rising; and 4. falling. These all sound a bit like somebody is singing. There is also a "neutral tone" which does not engage the singing voice and is said as you would speak something gently in English.

(See chapter 5 for more information on tones.)

CPSIA information can be obtained
at www.ICGtesting.com
Printed in the USA
LVOW13s1454090317

526677LV00025B/420/P